SCHOOL

D1150802

F IN SCHOOL

Summersdale Publishers Ltd
46 West Street
Chichester
West Sussex
PO19 1RP
UK

www.summersdale.com

Printed and bound in CPI Group (UK) Ltd, Croydon, CR0 4YY

ISBN: 978-1-84953-506-9

Substantial discounts on bulk quantities of Summersdale books are available to corporations, professional associations and other organisations. For details contact Nicky Douglas by telephone: +44 (0) 1243 756902, fax: +44 (0) 1243 786300 or email: nicky@summersdale.com.

F IN

SCHOOL

BLUNDERS, BACKCHAT AND BAD EXCUSES

Richard Benson

summersdale

Contents

Introduction

BACK TO SCHOOL!

If you've ever been to school and endured ridiculous rules, terrible teachers, mind-boggling maths problems and disgusting school dinners, then we're delighted to welcome you to *F in School,* where we run things a little differently. Here you'll learn classic comebacks to terrorise your teacher, giggle-worthy gags to baffle the most boisterous of bullies, excellent excuses to get yourself out of trouble (and PE!) and a whole host of hilarious answers to liven up your exam papers. Don't be fooled, though, we do have a few rules you must abide by during your time with us: 1) Laugh yourself silly, 2) Study hard if you want to achieve slacking success and 3) Bring your own lunch. Rather than exams, testing at *F in School* is self-evaluated, i.e. if you're chuckling and checking your phone, then you get an A! So take a seat somewhere comfortable (the sofa, the bus, the toilet), get out your books (just this one will do) and prepare for your first lesson...

Classroom

Chaos

Blackboard Banter &
Classroom Comebacks

Teacher: Are you chewing gum?

Student: Yeah, would you like some?

Teacher: Who's talking?

Student: Miss, are you hearing voices in your head again? Maybe you should see the nurse.

Teacher: Now, where are my board pens?

Student: Probably with your bored students.

Teacher: If I bought fifty loaves of bread for five pounds, what would each loaf be?

Student: Stale.

Teacher: Why have you got your finger in your ear?

Student: To stop things going in one ear and out the other!

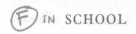

Art teacher: You're supposed to be drawing a monkey eating bananas, but you've only drawn a monkey.

Student: He ate all the bananas, Sir!

Classroom Chaos

Teacher: Why are you doing sit-ups in my classroom?

Student: You told me to show my working out.

Teacher: Where is your shirt?

Student: At home in my bed.

Teacher: Why?

Student: Yesterday, you told me to tuck it in!

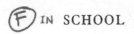

Teacher: Why are you not reading your mythology textbook?

Student: I would Miss, but I've got a Thor tooth.

Student: Can I use the bathroom?

Teacher: (correcting him) *May* I use the bathroom?

Student: Of course you can, Sir, why are you asking me?

Teacher: Which country has the most well-educated population?

Student: Mongolia.

Teacher: How do you know that?

Student: I read that the population was the least dense.

Teacher: Today, we're going to discuss your grammar.

Student: My grandma lives in a bungalow and loves knitting.

Teacher: Where are you going with that chair?

Student: You told me to take a seat.

Teacher: Why is there a pot of jam by the door?

Student: You told us to leave it a jar.

Miss Behavin'

Why was the protractor punished?

He didn't obey the ruler.

Why did the student get put in detention?

He'd given his teacher a hole punch.

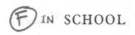

What do you call a dinosaur that's good at maths?

Pythagosaurus.

Why did the student give her teacher furniture polish?

She wanted to improve her marks.

Why did the teacher take her class to a cricket match?

She thought it would improve their test scores.

What branch of maths studies women's underwear?

Alge-bra.

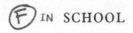

Knock knock

Who's there?

Broken Pencil.

Broken Pencil who?

Nevermind.
It's pointless.

What did the tailor say to the Classics teacher with the torn trousers?

Euripides?

Why did the students think their teacher was a ghost?

He kept saying he'd go through what was on the board.

Why did the pupil keep bringing scissors to school?

He was trying to cut class.

Why did the jelly bean start going to school?

He wanted to become a Smartie.

What did the maths teacher eat for his lunch?

Pi.

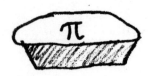

Why was the maths book always depressed?

It couldn't figure out how to solve all its problems.

Superb!

Why did the student take his calculator to every class?

He knew he could count on it.

La-di Tardy

Sorry I'm late, Miss...

"All the signs on the way to school said 'Go Slow'."

"My alarm was drowned out by my snoring."

"My spirit was here on time, but my body just took a while to catch up."

"I had to go and milk the cow for my mooosli."

"But you normally tell me to take my time."

"I wanted to treat you to an easy morning."

"I saw on the news there's a shortage of teachers so I thought you might not be here."

"But you know what they say, 'Better late than never!'"

"I'm actually just really early for tomorrow."

iPhone, Therefore I Am

When you get caught in class using your mobile, just say…

"This is an iPhone, not a 'you' phone."

"I have a gadget attachment disorder. Without my phone, I might die."

"I'm just reading up on the latest parliamentary reforms on school discipline."

"I'm tweeting about how great this class is."

"You don't expect me to ask a girl out by speaking to her face, do you?"

"Before you send me to the head, you *have* to watch this cat video on YouTube."

"I'm Instagramming your class to try and make it look cool."

"I'm adding you as a friend on Facebook."

"I'm doing some vital thumb exercises."

"It's not well – I'm trying to massage it better."

No Dog? No Prob!

Pup-free answers to the question, 'Where's your homework?'

"My python ate it, and my little brother."

"MI5 agents came and confiscated it as evidence."

"It's being published and will be out in November."

"A wizard accosted me on my walk to school and demanded I hand it over."

"If I mentioned aliens, would you believe me?"

[While pointing to your head] "It's all in here, Sir."

"My mum forgot to buy groceries, so I fed it to my younger sister."

"On my blog with the rest of my personal thoughts."

"Don't you remember? I gave it to you already. Maybe you should see the doctor."

Named & Shamed

Classic names from the world's most ridiculous register

Why didn't Mr Lee's boy turn up for school?

Because he was Paul Lee.

Anita Hogg?

I'll hug you, Miss, for a tenner!

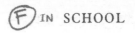

Since he bought glasses, Seymore Klearly has been top of the class!

Hugh Singh?

Why do I have to sing? You always pick on me!

Has anyone seen Mike Hardy?

It's on the back of your chair, Sir.

Homework

Assignment: Research and draw your family tree.

Assignment: Create a useful questionnaire to gauge your class's opinion.

1) How much are you enjoying this lesson?
☐ More than PE
☐ Less than PE
☐ I didn't realise we were supposed to enjoy it.

2) What's your favourite subject?
☐ Lunch
☐ The one where we use clay
☐ This one, of course. What is this one?

3) What do you think about homework?
☐ I don't think about it.
☐ unnecessary torture.
☐ All of the above.

Classroom Chaos

Assignment: Prepare a meal for your family and write about it (be sure to include all the ingredients).

Assignment: Interview an elderly relative about life in the wake of the Second World War. Report your findings.

I spoke to my nan and she said 'Are you calling me old?' Then she went on to tell me that things were a lot different back then. 'For one,' she said, 'school teachers didn't make us do stupid assignments like this one.' She described life as 'down at heel,' which I think means they did a lot of sitting, and everyone ate something called 'rations' which I think must be some old-fashioned kind of bacon.

Exam Time!
Part 1

bored
bored
bored
bored

Subject: **Science**

On a nature walk, where will you find humus?

If you go past a supermarket, it's in the chiller cabinet by the coleslaw.

What is the most powerful light source known to man?

Light Sabers.

Why do we put salt on the roads when it snows?

To make the tarmac taste better.

Why did Archimedes shout 'Eureka' when he stepped into the bath?

Because he smelt really bad and he was always talking to himself.

What does the 'law of gravity' refer to?

I don't know, but it sounds very serious

What's the difference between red blood cells and white blood cells?

Some are red,

Others are white.

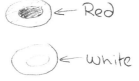

What are minerals?

Rules that are less important than major rules.

What is a thermal conductor?

A man who leads an orchestra in long johns.

What are the characteristics of a permeable rock?

It has curly hair.

Subject: ......**Maths**.........................

What kind of angle is this?

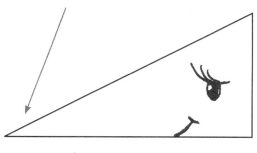

A cute angle

In a supermarket one tin of tuna costs 47p. How many tins can you buy with £2.83?

It depends - do they have a two for one deal going on?

How many dimensions does this cube have?

Two. I can't see the third because I left my 3D glasses at home.

Exam Time! Part 1

Describe the characteristics of a triangular prism.

A place with a pointed roof where bad people are locked up.

How do we know this angle is a right angle?

Because a left angle looks like this.

L

41

Saved by the Bell

Cafeteria Capers

Why does the cafeteria clock run slow?

Every day it goes back four seconds.

Why were the school children scared of the dinner lady?

They'd heard she battered fish, whipped cream, and beat eggs.

Student: Why aren't there any bananas?

Dinner lady: I guess they slipped my mind.

Why was the jelly self-conscious?

She had a bit of a wobble.

Why was the tomato struggling in PE class?

He couldn't ketchup.

Teacher: Why are you crying into your coffee?

Other teacher: Because I'm on cafeteria duty.

Why did the custard cry?

Because she saw the apple crumble.

Why was the peanut butter late?

She got stuck in the jam.

Why did the lettuce blush?

Because it saw the salad dressing.

What did the dinner lady say when she'd had enough?

I can't curry on!

Why was the class confused at the aquarium?

None of the fish had fingers.

Dinner lady: Why are you kicking your chips around the cafeteria?

Student: We're playing potato croquette!

What did one blackberry say to the other?

Why do people keep picking on me?

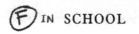

Bully to You!

What do bullies eat for lunch?

Knuckle sandwiches.

What do bullies drink with their sandwiches?

Grape punch.

Why did the student stop wearing red?

He didn't want to aggravate the bully.

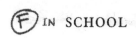

Why did the new kid steer clear of Bruce in the playground?

He'd heard he beat everyone in maths.

Why didn't the student stand up to the bully?

His teacher told him to sit down.

Why did the student become a bully?

Because his football coach told him he was a really good kicker.

Why did the student put his head in the toilet?

Because the bully was off sick that day.

Why did the students start carrying credit cards?

So the bully couldn't steal their lunch money.

Why did the bully kick the classroom computer?

He was booting up the system.

What do bullies have at the end of their sleeves?

Fisticuffs.

What's a bully's favourite thing in the gym?

The pummel horse.

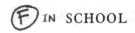

Break-Time Buffoonery

What did the horse chestnut seed say to his teacher when he was caught hitting his best friend?

It's not a big deal, Miss. We're just playing Conkers.

What do you call a kangaroo carrying a bottle of whisky?

Hop Scotch.

What game do mice play at break-time?

Hide and Squeak.

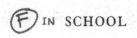

Three girls were walking through the playground carrying a rope. The teacher stopped them and said, 'Shouldn't you be on your way to the maths block?'

'No, Sir,' one girl replied. 'We're going to skip class.'

Why did the student hit the bully back?

She thought they were playing tag.

Why was the fizzy drink feeling queasy?

He'd just played Spin the Bottle.

Why did the kids end up in the pond?

They were playing leap frog.

Before the Whistle

Think skipping is a fun way to spend your break-time? Why not try going for the world record for most skips in one minute. It currently stands at 332 – the record was set by British skipper Beci Dale who smashed the existing record in 2009. Ropes at the ready!

Did you know that the largest packet of crisps ever made weighed 52 kg and measured 1.79 m tall by 1.21 m wide? The world record was set by Seabrook Potato Crisps Ltd, in Bradford, West Yorkshire in 2004.

The word for 'chocolate' comes from the Aztec word 'Xocolatl', which translates as 'bitter water' – it doesn't quite have the same ring to it though!

Smashing conkers around is a serious business in Northamptonshire where the World Conker Championships have taken place every year since 1965.

Exam Time!
Part 2

Subject: .....**English**.....................................

What word would you use to describe your mother's sister?

Fat.

63

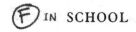

Summarise Hamlet's famous soliloquy.

He didn't know what pencil to use –
2B or not 2B.

What does Antonym mean?

I don't know what he means but you've spelt his name wrong, Miss.

Write the longest sentence you can, using appropriate punctuation.

50 years to life.

Use the word 'fascinate' in a sentence without changing the tense.

We bought my dad a shirt for his birthday. It had ten buttons, but because of his belly he was only able to fascinate

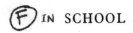

Define and give an example of an oxymoron.

An idiot who looks like a
bull — my Uncle Harry.

In *The Tempest*, why does Ariel sing into Gonzalo's ear?

She's a mermaid
and wants to
be a human.

Exam Time! Part 2

Subject: **Music**

In music, if 'f' stands for 'forte' what does 'ff' stand for?

Eighty.

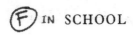

What is an operetta?

> The person in the
> switchboard who works
> the phones.

A high level of dissonance is often found in what type
of music.

> The kind that hurts
> people's ears.

Commonly found in jazz, what are blue notes?

Really sad short letters.

What does it mean if a note has an accent?

That it's written in another language

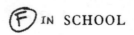

The tempo of a piece of music tells you the underlying speed, what does the pulse tell you?

If it's alive.

In music, what does andante mean?

How well cooked the pasta is

Terrible Teachers

Educator Eponyms

The names you wish your teacher had...

HEAD TEACHER
Tanya Hide

PE
Lee Ping

HISTORY
Luke Ingback

CHEMISTRY
Ben Senberner

PHILOSOPHY
Frida Mind

SINGING
Bell Canto

MODERN LANGUAGES
Gaynor Newtung

MATHS
Adam Upp

Terrible Teachers

ATHLETICS
Betty Winns

ECONOMICS
Iona Bank

CLASSICS
Harry Stottle

MATHS
Harry Thematick

SCHOOL INSPECTOR
Juno Eneething

PALAEONTOLOGY
Terry Dactill

HOME ECONOMICS
Wilma Kaykryse

RELIGION
Xavier Sole

GERMAN STUDIES
Heinz Svy

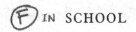

Detention Distractions

Ways to pass the time in the Sin Bin:

Work on that knitting project you've been meaning to get off the ground.

Practise your carving skills on the desk.

Learn to yodel.

Start a gang with your fellow inmates.

Question the on-duty teacher about their love life.

Play rubbish-bin basketball.

Meditate.

Fine-tune your ways to not get caught next time.

Eat a chocolate bar without using your hands.

Tunnel to freedom.

Get Me Outta Here!

Things to say to get you out of detention damnation!

"Can you smell burning?"

"I'm allergic to silence and small spaces."

"The voices in my head say I shouldn't be here."

"My head's itchy."

"I ate a curry at lunch and I've got really bad wind."

"I'm going to the loo and I might be a while."

"I think imprisonment of pupils is illegal – I'd like to speak to my lawyer."

"Can I serve double-time next week instead?"

"I've just had a premonition."

"That clock is definitely running slow."

"I need to go home now to feed my aardvark."

Parental Persuasion

Don't tell your mum and dad the real reason you were detained, these lies are way more fun!

"I took the fall for the other guy."

"I was on an undercover assignment for the school newspaper to see how students in detention are treated."

"I think I was set up."

"My teacher sent me so the naughty kids could see how an exemplary student behaves."

"I just really wanted the extra time to study."

"Only by being at the bottom, can you truly rise to the top."

"Detention is an essential part of the school experience."

"All my friends were going, and I didn't want to miss out."

"You're always telling me I should find an interest – I think detention might be my 'thing'."

Teacher Ticklers

Knock knock!

Who's there?

Teacher.

Teacher who?

Teacher-selves something for once. I'm taking the day off.

Knock knock!

Who's there?

Miss.

Miss who?

Miss-behaving will not be tolerated in my classroom.

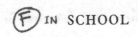

Knock knock!

Who's there?

Prince.

Prince who?

Prince-ipal's coming, everyone shut up!

Terrible Teachers

Knock knock!

Who's there?

Carrie.

Carrie who?

Carrie on working,
while I go and get a coffee.

Why did the teacher bring a tennis racket to class?

He wanted his students to ace the test.

How do you comfort an English teacher?

There, their, they're.

What's a head teacher's favourite nation?

Expla-nation.

Why did the students come to class in their football shirts?

They heard there was a substitute.

Why was the science teacher fired?

He left the Bunsen burners on.

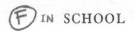 IN SCHOOL

Where do teachers eat their dinner?

At their times table.

Why did the teacher give up drinking?

She was sick of all the wine-ing.

Exam Time!

Part 3

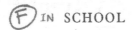 IN SCHOOL

Subject: Geography

How can you tell where a river is on an Ordnance Survey Map?

It's the bit that's wet.

What is the word that describes land masses such as Asia, Europe and North America?

Incontinent

What does the Beaufort scale measure?

How beautiful a French castle is.

What causes heavy rain?

Too much fast food.

What is commonly found at the start of a river?

Sauce

What kind of wildlife would you expect to see in Antarctica?

ants

Deserts can be hot or cold. Name a hot desert and a cold desert.

Hot desert - apple crumble
        with custard
Cold desert - jelly and
        ice cream

Name an expanse of salty water that's smaller than an ocean.

A tear.

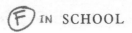

If a coastal arch collapses, what word would describe the remaining rock?

Lonely.

What is a continental plate?

Moussaka.

Which part of a glacier is known as the snout?

The part it sniffs with.

What are fossil fuels used for?

Powering dinosaurs.

Subject: ....**Art**..................................

What should you do to make sure the clay stays moist between art lessons?

Spit on it.

What do you make if you're a milliner?

Less money than
a billiner.

'Throwing' is one method use to make pottery – name
another.

Catching

What else might you expect to find inside an Egyptian pyramid, other than mummies?

Daddies

What are contours?

Coach holidays for prisoners.

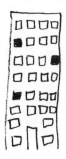

Name two different artist's materials.

1. Chalk
2. Cheese

What kinds of artists use collage?

The kind who passed all
their exams at school,

Sporting

Behaviour

Amused & Excused

The funniest ways to tell your PE teacher you're just not feeling up to it.

THE LAST MINUTE

When there's no time for a letter and a sports lesson sneaks up on you, simply say:

I will not be attending PE today because...

"I ate my sports kit."
"I am on the run and this just seems like an unnecessary use of energy."
"I literally have two left feet."
"I'm choking."
"I ate the fish at lunch."
"I've lost all the feeling in my left arm."
"My ears are bleeding... again."
"I'm saving myself for the Olympics."

THE ALL-ROUNDER

Dear [Insert your teacher's name]

I am unable to attend your PE class today/forever [delete as appropriate] for one of the following reasons:

[Please tick at least one]

- ☐ My professional coach doesn't want me to be influenced by any outside training.
- ☐ I believe I receive enough 'physical education' from the school bullies.
- ☐ My parents' don't want their taxes to go towards me diving in the mud.
- ☐ My sweat glands are broken.
- ☐ I'm allergic to coloured bibs.
- ☐ My new religion forbids any activity that involves a stick or a ball.
- ☐ I hate hockey.
- ☐ I found a magic lamp, and never doing PE again was one of my wishes.
- ☐ I'm not sure you really understand the offside rule.
- ☐ I'm averse to stretching (unless it's when I've just got out of bed).

Yours sincerely and not in the slightest bit sarcastically,
[Insert name here]

THE DOCTOR, DOCTOR

Dear [Insert your teacher's name],

I am writing to you about [insert your name]. I am his/her family GP, and I have some serious concerns about his/her health that I felt compelled to share with you. Over the last six months he/she has been coming to see me every week about a crippling ball phobia. He/she has been waking almost every night, terrified by ball-related nightmares (oftentimes involving balls of the football variety, but occasionally tennis and hockey too). Despite various therapies, including hypnosis, we have been unable to cure this deep-seated phobia. I urge you to remove [insert name] from all lessons involving balls, of any nature, as I feel that it will only compound the problem. Please do not mention this to [insert name] as I fear it will only make him/her worse.

Yours medically,
Doctor Ivor Cure

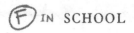

THE AWOL-LY

Dear [Insert your teacher's name]

I am writing to let you know that I will no longer be attending any PE lessons for the rest of the year. I have spoken to my spiritual leader, Guru B. Urself, and he has advised me to remove the trivial pursuit of traditional sporting competition from my life and focus on my inner champion. To do this, I shall spend the Physical Education portion of the school week sitting in a meditative state, eating foods that nourish my soul (like chocolate and chicken nuggets), and watching TV shows that bring me true happiness.

May you one day find such inner peace for yourself.

From,
My subconscious

THE SERIOUS INCIDENT

Dear [Insert your teacher's name]

There's been a serious incident, which means our son/ daughter [delete as appropriate] will not be able to attend your PE class today. Without going into too many gory details, it involved a lawnmower, our child's foot and a hedgehog. We hope he/she will be able to resume PE lessons next week, all being well. Although the doctor said there is a chance that he/she will be terrified of grass and feet for the rest of his/her life, making most of your sport curriculum off limits.

Yours,
Mr and Mrs [insert name]

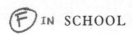
Sporty Shenanigans

Why did the gooseberry look sad in PE lessons?

Because he always got picked last.

Sporting Behaviour

PE teacher: There's no I in team!

Student: Is that why I'm never on it?

What's a fish's least favourite sport?

Netball.

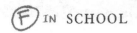

Why did the boys catch the bus after PE?

They wanted to avoid the coach.

PE teacher: Why are you behaving like an idiot?

Student: I thought we were playing follyball.

Sporting Behaviour

How did the caterpillar drown?

He was trying to swim butterfly.

Why did the swimming captain eat so much chicken?

He thought it would improve his breaststroke.

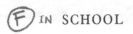

Why did the school ref get called to the head teacher's office?

Because he was the whistle-blower.

PE teacher: Where have you been? The lesson's nearly over.

Student: I was practising my long-distance running and I made it all the way home and back again.

Why do rugby players need calculators?

So they can do conversions.

PE teacher: Why do you keep leaving the pitch, Lee?

Student: Because you're always shouting 'Go Lee! Go Lee!'

Why did the student bring his LP collection to the competition?

He wanted to break some records.

Sporting Behaviour

Why did the students run towards the church?

They were competing in a steeplechase.

Why did the student bring soap and water to the cricket match?

He wanted to prevent a sticky wicket.

What's a cow's favourite discipline?

Herdles.

What do you call a trampolining sheep?

A woolly jumper.

Final Whistle

The fastest sporting hit of all time belongs not to a golf ball, tennis ball or ice hockey puck, but to the humble shuttlecock. Malaysia's Tan Boon Heong hit one at 261.6 mph, that's almost 100 mph faster than the world's fastest tennis serve. Speedy!

It's widely believed that the Ancient Olympic Games were first held in 776 BC and only freeborn Greek men were allowed to participate. Oh, and all events required the competitors to be naked!

The world record for the loudest crowd roar at a sports stadium is held by Turkey's Galatasaray SK fans. In 2011, 49,488 of them cheered their way to victory, recording a sound level of 131.76 dB.

Here's a sport you probably haven't heard of – hurdling with swimming fins on! There's even a world record holder for the 100 metre hurdles – Germany's Christopher Irmscher, who completed the distance in 14.82 seconds.

Exam Time!
Part 4

Subject: ...........**P.E**............................

Explain the benefits of proteins.

People who are pro-teens make sure young people's opinions are taken seriously.

Name three benefits of regular training.

1) It's cheaper than driving.
2) You can read on the train.
3) They have a snack trolley.

What is the primary function of alveoli?

a dip for
potato wedges

How does your humerus differ from your fibula?

One's funny and the other lies a lot.

What is the primary function of hamstrings?

Keep the Sunday roast in one piece till you're ready to eat it.

How do you identify athlete's foot?

It's on the end of athlete's leg.

Why might a professional athlete take beta blockers?

If their current blockers aren't very good and they want some beta ones.

How does the 'cox' differ from the rest of a rowing team?

They eat a lot of apples during training.

How many different strokes do Olympic swimmers do in the Individual Medley?

Depends how many cats are by the pool.

Why do basketball players dribble close to the ground?

to reduce the chance of
their saliva getting on their
shorts.

Why would an uncontrolled jibe be dangerous while sailing?

It could offend the other
members of the crew.

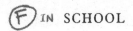

Subject: ....**History**.........................

Which of Henry VIII's wives was never imprisoned in the Tower of London?

Anne of Keys

How did the Romans transport water?

Via ducks

Where did the Vikings get the tar to waterproof their boats?

B ≠ Q

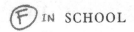

Define capital punishment.

When you get in trouble
for not putting a
capital letter at the
Start of a sentence

When Queen Elizabeth I came to the throne, what was
the first thing she did?

Sat down.

The Romans came from which modern country?

Romania.

Name the Russian mystic who was an advisor to the Romanov family.

Merlinsky

Why did the infamous 1605 Gunpowder Plot fail?

Someone forgot to bring the matches.

How did the introduction of the 'Spinning Mule' affect manufacturing in Great Britain during the Industrial Revolution?

There were more dancing donkeys to keep people happy.

If All
Else Fails

Neat Cheats

Naughty ways to get you straight As in exams:

Sit next to the smartest person and develop a stiff neck.

Wear magnifying glasses in place of your regular glasses.

Eat an entire textbook and head for the loos.

Tattoo the answers on your arms (or your thighs, if you're wearing shorts).

Bribe your teacher with fancy chocolates.

Learn to use your iPhone under the desk without looking down.

Develop X-ray vision.

Hire a nerd to hide under your desk and whisper the answers to you.

Create a version of semaphore using pencils to communicate with your friends.

Write as much information as you can on the back of your eraser.

I Like To Move It, Move It

Keep yourself active while you're stuck in the exam hall:

Demand a toilet break at least once every ten minutes (don't forget to discuss your weak bladder loudly before the exam starts).

When you're in the loo, do a series of squats to prevent the dreaded 'numb-bum' syndrome.

Drop your pen frequently, far from your desk, requiring a serious arm stretch.

If someone needs a ruler, practise your javelin throw as you make it sail across the exam hall.

Yawning uses a lot of muscles – do it loudly and often. Don't forget about your examiner – they need a workout too. Raise your hand at regular intervals (preferably when they've just sat down) so they can keep the blood pumping.

Congratulations, Graduates!

You've worked as little as possible, annoyed your teachers to breaking point and brought new levels of meaning to the word 'slacker'. If there were medals for such a cause, you would get them all. A master of excuses; a deliverer of awkward comebacks; a student of really wrong exam answers… you have excelled in all these and more. So don your ill-fitting gown, toss your crumpled cap carelessly into the air and celebrate your graduation from *F in School* – the only academic institution where lower learning is the order of the day, and there is no order in the day.

The Bored of Governors is proud
to announce that

_____

has graduated *summa cum laude*
from *F in School*!

Whether your school days are still dragging by, or are now just a blurry but traumatic memory, we'd love to hear your F in School stories!

Send them to **auntie@summersdale.com**, or find us on Facebook at **Summersdale Publishers** and on Twitter at **@Summersdale**.

www.summersdale.com